Autumn
Publishing

Published in 2017
by Autumn Publishing
Cottage Farm
Sywell
NN6 0BJ
www.igloobooks.com

LEO002 0517
2 4 6 8 10 9 7 5 3 1
ISBN 978-1-78810-667-2

The publisher would like to thank Alamy for permission to use the
following images: page 8 (left), ArteSub / Alamy Stock Photo; 10 (left),
Nature Picture Library / Alamy Stock Photo; 11 (bottom), WaterFrame
/ Alamy Stock Photo; 12 (centre), Alan Skyrme / Alamy Stock Photo; 12
(top), john t. fowler / Alamy Stock Photo; 12 (centre), blickwinkel / Alamy
Stock Photo; 17 (centre), blickwinkel / Alamy Stock Photo; 17 (bottom),
Minden Pictures / Alamy Stock Photo; 18 (top), All Canada Photos / Alamy
Stock Photo; 28 (bottom), Juniors Bildarchiv GmbH / Alamy Stock Photo;
28 (centre), Mircea Costina / Alamy Stock Photo; 29 (bottom), Alamy Stock
Photo. All other images provided by iStockphoto.com.

Cover designed by Richard Sykes
Interiors designed by Starry Dog Books

Printed and manufactured in China

OVER
100
FACTS FOR KIDS
KNIGHTS

Autumn
Publishing

The World of Knights

FACT 1 Hundreds of years ago, in a time called the Middle Ages, the best soldiers in Europe were called knights.

Knight

FACT 2 At the time, Europe was split up into lots of small kingdoms, which often fought each other.

FACT 3 Rulers of the kingdoms gave land and castles to their best knights. In return, the knights promised to fight for them.

FACT 4 A knight had to have his own horse, armour and weapons, so he could ride into battle.

FACT 5 Sometimes a knight lived with the lord he served, and helped to defend the lord's castle if it was attacked.

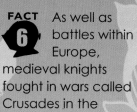

FACT 6 As well as battles within Europe, medieval knights fought in wars called Crusades in the Middle East and North Africa.

Europe and the Middle East

FACT 7 The Crusades were fought between 1096 and 1291.

FACT 8 Knights were warriors, but they also had to be kind and honourable, and protect their people.

Medieval fortress of Carcassonne, France

Knights' Weapons

FACT 9 Knights were equipped with weapons for fighting on horseback and on foot.

Knight with lance

FACT 10 When they were on horseback, knights carried long spears called lances.

FACT 11 The longest lances were about 4 m (14 ft) long, or as long as a small car.

Medieval weapons

FACT 12 If a knight was knocked off his horse, he continued to fight on foot.

FACT 13 Knights were trained to use lots of different types of weapons.

Swords and shields

FACT 14 Many knights carried shields for protection. They were usually made of wood with metal supports.

FACT 15 Knights' swords were generally about 70 cm (28 in) long. That's about the height of a 7-year-old child.

FACT 16 Some swords were up to 1.6 m (5 ft) long, and it took two hands to lift them.

FACT 17 Some knights used maces, heavy clubs with metal points.

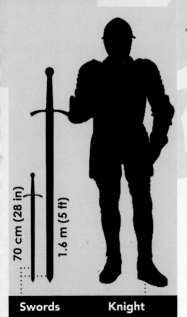

70 cm (28 in)

1.6 m (5 ft)

Swords   Knight

Mace

Knights' Armour

FACT 18 A knight's suit of armour was one of his most valuable and prized possessions.

Suit of armour

FACT 19 Armour was very expensive. Poor knights depended on their lords to pay for their armour.

Chain mail

FACT 20 Chain mail armour was made from lots of small metal rings linked together.

FACT 21 A helmet protected a knight's head. Some helmets had a visor that could be pulled down to cover the face.

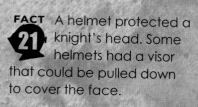
Helmet

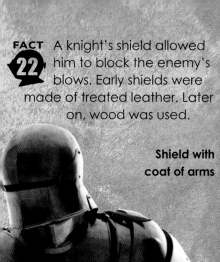

FACT 22 A knight's shield allowed him to block the enemy's blows. Early shields were made of treated leather. Later on, wood was used.

Shield with coat of arms

FACT 23 Plate mail was armour made from sheets of metal. It was much heavier and stronger than chain mail.

FACT 24 A knight's body was protected by a breastplate in front and a backplate behind.

FACT 25 Most knights wore a layer of padded clothing under their armour to stop it rubbing.

FACT 26 Knights had to be very strong to fight in armour. The whole suit weighed as much as a child.

Tournaments

FACT 27 Knights practised a range of fighting skills at competitions called tournaments.

FACT 28 Jousting was a contest in which two knights on horseback charged at each other.

FACT 29 Each knight tried to knock his opponent off his horse with his lance.

FACT 30 Knights who won jousting contests gained fame and honour.

FACT 31 The lances used for jousting were blunt, but knights could still get badly hurt.

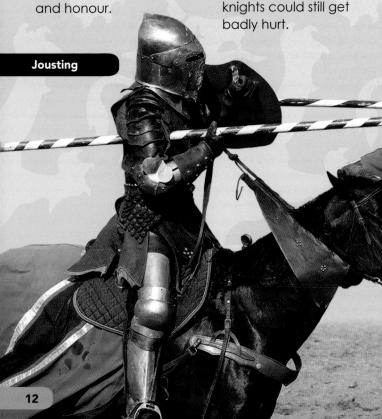

Jousting

Lady and knight

FACT 32 At tournaments, a lady sometimes gave a knight something to wear, such as a scarf. This was a sign that she wanted him to win.

FACT 33 Kings sometimes took part in jousts, but it's possible that his knights always let him win.

FACT 34 As well as jousting, there were contests in sword fighting and giant pretend battles.

Sword fighting

Life in the Middle Ages

FACT 35 Kings and queens were the most powerful people in the Middle Ages.

Richard I, King of England

FACT 37 The king owned all the land, and could give pieces of it to anyone he wanted – usually lords who were loyal to him.

FACT 39 Knights mostly served great lords. They lived with them, or on lands given to them to look after.

FACT 41 A knight's lands were worked by poor farm labourers called peasants or serfs. They worked very hard all year.

A king's castle

King

FACT 36 In wartime, kings were expected to lead their armies and fight alongside their knights.

Lords and ladies

FACT 38 Lords and their families lived in strong castles. The lord had power over the local people.

Knights

FACT 40 Other important people in the Middle Ages included priests and merchants.

Peasants

FACT 42 People worked for those above them (peasants worked for knights, knights for lords etc). This was called feudalism.

Castles

FACT 43 Kings, lords and their families lived in strong castles protected by thick stone walls.

The Great Hall

FACT 44 The Great Hall was the main room in the castle. It was used for large formal meals or banquets.

FACT 45 The lord of the castle held private meetings in a room called the solar.

FACT 46 The biggest castles were fortress towns. They had great stone walls enclosing houses, shops, stables, gardens and workshops.

FACT 47 At the centre of a castle was the keep. Defenders sheltered there if attackers broke through the walls.

Castle keep

Blacksmith

FACT 48 The large, open areas were used for practising weapons skills.

FACT 49 Every castle had a blacksmith. It was his job to make weapons, armour and horseshoes.

FACT 50 The horses were looked after in large stables.

Stables

FACT 51 Gardens were kept so that people could grow food if the castle was besieged (attacked for a long time).

Beynac castle, France

17

Under Siege

FACT 52 Before armies had gunpowder, it was almost impossible to break down a castle's walls.

FACT 53 Attackers who got close would try to bash their way through the gates with battering rams.

Battering ram

FACT 54 Siege towers were used by attacking armies to help soldiers climb over the tops of castle walls.

Siege tower

FACT 55 Inside a castle, archers fired arrows at the enemy through slits in the walls. The slits were easy to fire out of, but hard for the enemy to fire into.

FACT 56 Soldiers on the gate towers defended the gates by throwing down rocks and firing arrows.

Arrow slit seen from inside

FACT 57 If an attacking army was unable to force its way into a castle, it could besiege it instead. This was the easiest way to capture a castle.

FACT 58 A siege was when the enemy blocked a castle's gates so that no supplies could get in and no one could get out.

Castle under attack

FACT 59 A siege could last for several months. When the food in the castle ran out, the people inside had no choice but to surrender.

FACT 60 Many castles had a small, secret gate called a postern. During a siege, people could use this to slip in and out without being seen.

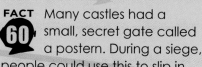

Postern

Types of Castle

FACT 61 Not all castles were giant stone structures. Early castles were simple wooden buildings.

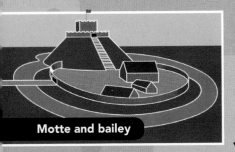

Motte and bailey

FACT 62 In a motte and bailey castle, the motte was a mound with a wooden keep on top.

FACT 63 The bailey was a large courtyard. It was surrounded by a high wooden fence to keep out attackers.

FACT 64 Castles were often built on high ground so that lookouts could see an enemy approaching from a distance.

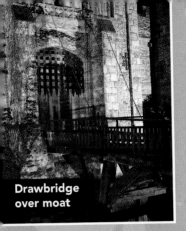

Drawbridge over moat

Hilltop castle

FACT 65 Some castles were surrounded by a moat, a deep ditch full of water.

FACT 66 A drawbridge could be lowered to allow people to cross the moat.

FACT 67 Castles on hills were harder to attack. Invaders had to climb uphill to get close, while defenders shot arrows at them.

FACT 68 Some of the biggest castles were built in the Middle East by invading Crusaders.

FACT 69 Knights living in enemy territory needed especially strong castles to keep them safe.

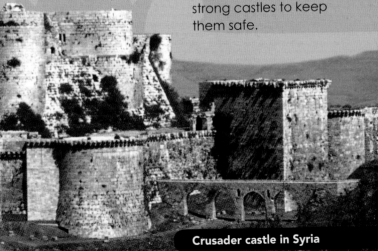

Crusader castle in Syria

Knights
and Stories

FACT 70 Stories about knights have been told for hundreds of years.

The sword in the stone

FACT 71 The legend of King Arthur tells of the heroic king and his knights of the Round Table, who kept Britain safe from invaders.

FACT 72 Arthur is said to have proved his right to the throne by pulling an enchanted sword out of a stone.

Sir Lancelot, knight of the Round Table

FACT 73 King Arthur's sword, Excalibur, was said to shine out light to blind his enemies. Its scabbard protected the king from dangerous wounds.

FACT 74 King Arthur was defeated when one of his own knights, Mordred, turned against him.

FACT 75 The stories about King Arthur are probably not true, but they may have been based on real events.

Joan of Arc

FACT 76 Joan of Arc is the heroine of many tales. This brave French knight led the army of France to victory over the English in 1430.

FACT 77 *The Song of Roland* is a famous poem about a heroic knight. Roland's sword, Durendal, could not be broken.

FACT 78 Roland was killed when he and his soldiers were ambushed by a much larger army.

Statue of Roland

Becoming a Knight

Lord and page

FACT 79 It took many years of training to become a knight.

FACT 80 Sons of noble families started their training at the age of 7. They were sent away to work as pages.

FACT 81 Pages had to deliver messages, clean weapons and learn how to use them.

FACT 82 At 13, pages became squires. A squire had to look after his master's horse and armour.

Knight and his squire

Knight keeping a vigil

FACT 83
Squires learned how to fight by watching and practising with their masters.

FACT 84
Squires had to ride into battle alongside their masters. It was a dangerous life.

FACT 85
If a squire did well, he would become a knight himself and be given his own horse and armour.

FACT 86
Before he was made a knight, the squire would spend a night in prayer. This was called a vigil.

FACT 87
Only a lord or king could make someone a knight.

Knighting ceremony

25

Medieval Armies

FACT 88 Knights were the most powerful soldiers, but they were only a small part of an army.

FACT 89 At the beginning of the Middle Ages, foot soldiers were mostly poor, untrained peasants.

FACT 90 Early foot soldiers fought with simple weapons such as farm tools and spears.

FACT 91 Later on, foot soldiers were given training and they had better weapons.

Peasant soldier

FACT 92 Archers were a vital part of many armies. They could attack from a distance, and their arrows could pierce a knight's armour.

Archers and foot soldiers

Longbow archer

FACT 93 Longbows were about 1.8 m (6 ft) long, or the height of a tall man.

FACT 94 Arrows fired from crossbows flew faster than arrows from longbows, but crossbows were harder to use and slower to load.

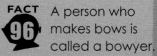

Crossbow archer

FACT 95 Laws in England said archers had to practise regularly, so they could fire quickly and accurately.

FACT 96 A person who makes bows is called a bowyer.

27

Heraldry

FACT 97 In battle, it was vital for knights to be able to tell friends from enemies. Knights wore coloured symbols to show who they were.

FACT 98 A knight's symbol was called his coat of arms. Studying coats of arms is called heraldry.

Knights on the battlefield

FACT 99 A knight's coat of arms was painted on his shield, so everyone could tell who he was, even in full armour.

FACT 100 Over time, coats of arms became more complicated. The design showed who a knight's parents were and who his king was.

Coats of arms

FACT 101 Heralds were experts in shields. They knew each knight's design, and made sure no two knights had the same coat of arms.

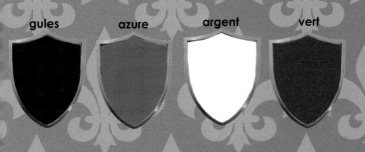

gules   azure   argent   vert

FACT 102 Heraldry has special names for the colours and patterns used on coats of arms.

FACT 103 A knight's surcoat or tunic displayed a simple version of his coat of arms.

FACT 104 Even horses sometimes wore the colours of their knight.

FACT 105 Some families today, especially royalty, still have heraldic coats of arms.

Surcoats and shields